Teaching Languages
in Blended Synchronous
Learning Classrooms

Also from Georgetown University Press

*A Practical Guide to Integrating Technology
into Task-Based Language Teaching*
Marta González-Lloret

*Brave New Digital Classroom:
Technology and Foreign Language Learning*
Third Edition
Robert J. Blake and Gabriel Guillén

*Integrating the Digital Humanities into the Second
Language Classroom: A Practical Guide*
Melinda A. Cro

Teaching Languages in Blended Synchronous Learning Classrooms

A Practical Guide

Alba Girons and Nicholas Swinehart

GEORGETOWN UNIVERSITY PRESS

The publisher is not responsible for third-party websites or their content. URL links were active at time of publication.

Library of Congress Cataloging-in-Publication Data

Names: Girons, Alba, author. | Swinehart, Nicholas, author.
Title: Teaching Languages in Blended Synchronous Learning Classrooms :
    A Practical Guide / Alba Girons, Nicholas Swinehart.
Description: Washington, DC: Georgetown University Press, 2019. | Includes
    bibliographical references.
Identifiers: LCCN 2019040012 (print) | LCCN 2019040013 (ebook) |
    ISBN 9781626168060 (paperback) | ISBN 9781626168077 (ebook)
Subjects: LCSH: Language and languages—Study and teaching. | Blended learning.
Classification: LCC P53.G5 2019 (print) | LCC P53 (ebook) | DDC 428.0071—dc23
LC record available at https://lccn.loc.gov/2019040012
LC ebook record available at https://lccn.loc.gov/2019040013

♾ This book is printed on acid-free paper meeting the requirements of the American National Standard for Permanence in Paper for Printed Library Materials.

21 20   9 8 7 6 5 4 3 2   First printing

Printed in the United States of America.
Cover design by Pam Pease.

Cover image courtesy of Georgetown University. Photograph by Paul Jones. This blended synchronous classroom includes students from the School of Foreign Service at both the Washington, DC, and Qatar campuses.

Contents

Illustrations

Introduction

IN THE AUTUMN of 2016, three professors from separate universities, one in the United States and two in Canada, organized a graduate seminar course in Chinese history that tested the limits of online education. The course would be cotaught by the three professors, as well as by guest lecturers throughout the term and would include students from each of the three universities—and a number of others. In total, more than twenty students from five different institutions in the United States and Canada attended weekly lecture and discussion sessions held synchronously via videoconference, with most students attending from a classroom with peers and some from a laptop at home. For the professor giving that day's lecture, this meant facilitating discussion between two audiences: those in the classroom and those on the screen.

The scenario above is an example of blended synchronous learning (BSL), which combines face-to-face and remote students in one synchronous environment. While far more complex than most BSL environments, which typically involve fewer instructors, students, institutions, and locations, this example illustrates the way that BSL provides opportunities that were not possible before the widespread use of affordable conferencing technologies. The ability to combine on-campus and online students offers solutions for a wide range of needs and motivations among universities, academic programs, instructors, and individual students. This represents a next step in the evolution of teaching and learning in the digital age and a blurring of the boundaries between "face-to-face" and "online" students because all students in a BSL classrooms are both online and face-to-face simultaneously, though the terms are still used by convention to distinguish between the two groups.

In 2014, the authors of this book—one a Catalan language instructor and one an instructional technologist—began participating in a course-sharing system that allowed students from other institutions to participate in our language classes remotely. This blending of face-to-face and online students into one synchronous environment was an entirely new challenge for us. While we sought advice from peers at other institutions who had experience in these environments, published information was scarce and hard to find—especially when we did not even know what to call it. This is the book we wish we had when we began this endeavor: a concise guide to the many things instructors, administrators, and technical support staff should consider when beginning to open up their face-to-face language classes to online students. We hope this book will serve as a beginner's guide that is useful to language instructors who need to increase enrollments by opening up their courses to new populations, staff and administrators whose institutions are adopting blended synchronous courses, and teacher training programs that wish to prepare their students for this exciting and challenging environment.

The book is divided into three parts. Chapter 1 contextualizes BSL, offering definitions, benefits, challenges, and contexts. Chapter 2 discusses the differing BSL environments, including the technology, layouts, and training needed before implementation. Finally, chapter 3 reviews the pedagogical challenges of BSL. Therein, we discuss group dynamics, how students provide input and feedback, and examples of activities, and we offer a section on smart tricks for instructors that are new to BSL teaching.

1

Contextualizing Blended
Synchronous Learning

THIS SYNCHRONOUS MIXTURE of learning modalities has been referred to by several names, including "synchromodal" (Bell, Cain, and Sawaya 2013) and "synchronous hybrid" (Butz et al. 2014), with "blended synchronous" (Hastie et al. 2010) emerging as the most consistently used label. Definitions are similarly varied, including "the integration of physical classroom and cyber classroom settings using synchronous learning to enable unlimited connectivity for teachers and students from any part of the world" (Hastie et al. 2010, 10) and "learning and teaching where remote students participate in face-to-face classes by means of rich-media synchronous technologies such as video conferencing, web conferencing, or virtual worlds" (Bower et al. 2014, 11). In an attempt to further distill the definition to its most integral components, we define BSL as technology-mediated learning environments where face-to-face and remote students are joined synchronously.

What does this look like in practice? On one end there is usually a fairly traditional classroom—an instructor and face-to-face students gathered around tables or desks, a surface for the instructor to write on—with the addition of conferencing technology that allows remote students on the other end to participate in the class. This means that even the physical environment is blended in a way that forces instructors to direct attention to both the physical and technological components simultaneously. On the other end(s), remote students may be gathered in a similar conferencing-equipped classroom on their local campus or may join individually from a personal device, depending on the context. Each student, regardless of physical location, is a full participant in the course and can receive equal course credit.

Benefits and Challenges

BSL environments offer benefits to a wide range of stakeholders. At the institutional level, BSL allows universities to make efficient use of limited resources. Some institutions may be able to offer one course to students at multiple campuses, rather than running multiple sections with smaller enrollment. In other cases, universities who are unable to hire faculty to teach a given course may be able to "share" that course with another institution, typically as a result of mutually beneficial partnerships. Academic programs, particularly at the graduate level, can make their programs more accessible to students who may not otherwise be able to attend due to geographic or schedule constraints. For instructors who consistently struggle with low enrollment, BSL offers opportunities to open courses up to new populations of students who need such specialized offerings. Finally, BSL can enable students to participate in highly specialized courses at other campuses or institutions that would otherwise not be available to them, as well as engage in a more interactive and dynamic online learning experience.

The benefits of BSL come at the cost of significant challenges and demands on resources in terms of administration, technology, and pedagogy. The administrative challenges come in part from logistical concerns from having students in multiple locations, and they are exacerbated when these students are enrolled at different campuses or separate institutions. Technological challenges include selecting hardware and software, integrating the technology into well-designed learning spaces, training instructors and students to use equipment effectively, and providing ongoing support and evaluation. While these administrative and technological challenges are formidable, particularly in the early stages of BSL implementation, there are many workable solutions for institutions to choose from, depending on their needs and resources. The pedagogical challenges of teaching two (or more) separate audiences simultaneously, however, are even more numerous and lack easily identifiable solutions. As a result, the majority of this book is devoted to discussing pedagogical challenges and strategies for overcoming them.

Example Contexts

Examples where BSL has been implemented are as diverse as the many needs and contexts of institutions, multi-institution organizations, and individual programs, and each context presents different motivations, challenges, and considerations. What follows is not an exhaustive history of BSL environments but rather a number of contexts representative of typical uses of BSL.

Within a Single Institution

The most common use of BSL is within a single course or program where all students are enrolled at the same institution. Some students attend class in an on-campus classroom, while other remote students (either permanently or temporarily away from campus) attend via conferencing technologies. These situations typically align with more traditional contexts of online courses or distance education, with BSL serving as a tool to further remove barriers between remote and face-to-face students. This can sometimes be used for relatively large lecture classes where remote students have the option of either viewing the lecture synchronously or watching a recording asynchronously (Popov 2009). However, BSL is most beneficial for smaller groups where interaction among all participants is key. Graduate programs are one of the most common users of BSL (e.g., Bell et al. 2016), which offers solutions for maintaining engagement among students who are often geographically dispersed. Using BSL in smaller courses or programs like these allows for more interaction than asynchronous online sections or activities, enabling graduate students to build and maintain relationships with faculty and within their cohort of peers.

Multiple Campuses within One System

Institutions with multiple campuses, like large state university systems, can at times use BSL to offer courses taught at one campus to students attending other campuses. One example relevant to language instruction is the University of Wisconsin's Collaborative Language Program, established in 1998 and serving approximately 300 students per semester (University of Wisconsin n.d.). This program allows students at branch campuses to learn languages like Hmong, Japanese, and Russian, where materials and even instructors can be difficult to find. Compared to partnerships between separate institutions, the administration of these courses is relatively streamlined in terms of coordinating enrollments, classroom space, technology, and support staff.

Cross-institutional Partnerships

A third context for BSL is partnerships that allow students from one institution to enroll in courses offered by another, typically while attending online from their home campus. This represents the most complex use of BSL and will be discussed in greater detail in chapter 2. Two language-specific examples are the Shared Course Initiative between Columbia University, Yale University, and Cornell University, and the Big Ten Academic Alliance's CourseShare program. Both these programs make a wide range of languages available to a large number of students who would otherwise not have access to such offerings, but they require a significant investment of resources—financial, technological, and human—at each institution.

Research

A growing body of research has served to increase the visibility and availability of information on blended synchronous instruction. Initial problems regarding BSL research included a lack of common vocabulary: as noted above, researchers had used several different terms to refer to face-to-face and remote students in the same class. At present, BSL research appears to be in transition from the early stages of descriptive case studies to more analytical research tied to theories and methodologies of teaching and learning. This section briefly highlights some common strands of research regarding BSL environments.

Case Studies

By far the largest amount of published research on BSL is case studies that describe the practices of one or more instances of BSL, often including findings in terms of best practices and recommendations (e.g., Bell et al. 2016; Cain, Sawaya, and Bell 2013; Chakraborty and Victor 2004; Cunningham 2014; Rogers et al. 2003; Roseth, Akcaoglu, and Zellner 2013;

Szeto 2015; Wang and Huang 2018). One particular example is Bower et al.'s (2014) *Blended Synchronous Learning: A Handbook for Educators*, which presents seven different case studies from a range of contexts and a cross-case analysis of student perceptions, technology, pedagogy, cognitive load, and institutional factors.

Perceptions of Students and Instructors

Another large group of studies investigates the perceptions of students and instructors on their experiences in BSL environments (e.g., Bower et al. 2014; Conklin 2017; Conklin, Oyarzun, and Barreto 2017; Cunningham 2014; Stewart, Harlow, and DeBacco 2011; Szeto 2014). One key finding for instructors is the added cognitive load when dealing with two seperate groups of students in one learning environment (Bower et al. 2014; Conklin, Oyarzun, and Barreto 2017). Results for students are varied and at times contradictory, but these studies highlight the fact that both groups have advantages and disadvantages that can affect their satisfaction and perspectives. For example, online students tend to have higher intrinsic motivation due to enrolling in a course that may not otherwise be available to them (Conklin 2017), but they are isolated from their instructor and the physical classroom and may not have the same ability to speak as freely as their face-to-face peers. These face-to-face students, on the other hand, may feel uncomfortable having remote students in their class (Conklin 2017) and that their instructor is giving more attention to the remote group (Szeto 2014).

Comparative Studies of Learning Outcomes

Another strand of BSL research, and one that remains underdeveloped, is studies that compare the experiences and outcomes of face-to-face students with those of online students. The goal is to ensure that both groups attain equal (or at least equitable) learning outcomes and identify factors that may favor one group over the other, so that those factors can be mitigated in future implementations. Szeto (2014) found that the two groups experienced different learning effects, with the remote group perceived to have received more attention from the instructor, but similar learning outcomes. Butz et al. (2014) similarly found few significant differences between the two groups in needs satisfaction, motivation, or perceived success.

Models and Frameworks

Several studies use findings from their own and other research to present models and frameworks for BSL implementation. In designing the layout of BSL environments, Bell, Cain, and Sawaya (2013) and Hastie et al. (2010) both provide models and illustrations for possible combinations of students and instructors in the physical and online spaces. Szeto and Cheng (2016, 500) focus on factors that occur during course meetings in their framework of interactions, examining how interaction frequency, direction, and patterns are affected by the blended social presence. Bower et al.'s (2015, 14) Blended Synchronous Learning Design Framework combines these elements into a matrix of recommendations for pedagogy, technology, and logistics at the presage (design), process (implementation), and product (outcome) stages.

BSL and Less Commonly Taught Languages

As mentioned above, language programs are relatively heavy users of BSL in intra- or cross-institutional settings. This is in part because the needs of language teaching, particularly with less commonly taught languages (LCTLs), and the benefits of BSL overlap in such a way that BSL and LCTL instruction are a uniquely well-suited pairing.

Small programs, a lack of published textbooks and other materials, lack of visibility within and among institutions, and low or variable enrollments are some of the most frequent challenges facing LCTLs. This variability in enrollments makes it difficult for programs to consolidate and strengthen, at times threatening an LCTL's survival within an institution. Also, not all LCTLs can be offered in all universities—nor should that be the objective. Some students, especially graduate students, might choose their university based on the availability of a specific language, but often students from an educational institution only have access to a short list of languages, with a very limited number of LCTLs (if any).

LCTL programs often consist of a single instructor, which adds fragility to the program since the survival of the program is linked to the presence of that instructor at the university. At the same time these programs can become isolated, with few possibilities for the single instructor to exchange pedagogical insights and materials with peers who teach the same language. Therefore, other than the administration's willingness to offer an LCTL, a strong language program requires a qualified person who can teach it and maintain enough demand to sustain it.

BSL offers several affordances that can help overcome these difficulties. BSL allows institutions to share their courses with other universities, improving enrollments and the ability to offer a wider range of courses to their students. From universities' perspectives (both administration and faculty), BSL can help raise the number of enrollments of LCTL programs, allowing students from peer institutions to enroll in their courses. When sharing courses, institutions can be more creative in order to accommodate the needs of peer universities and their students: attracting students interested in languages that are not offered at their home campus; sharing advanced courses with students whose universities only have lower levels; or designing entire programs in collaboration with other institutions so that students from each university can take part in a program that is co-taught at each campus.

This collaboration among universities allows programs to grow and strengthen, offering courses aimed at higher proficiency levels, a wider variety of courses, and specialized courses in specific topics (e.g., cinema, art, language for the professions, reading for specific purposes). Courses that might have been difficult to create when the available pool of students was just a single university's population can become more feasible with a larger population when the course is offered to several universities at the same time.

When creating partnerships among universities, instructors can also benefit from working with peers from the same language. As stated above, LCTL programs are often run by one instructor; with BSL, instructors from different universities can work together when developing programs, reflecting on their programs and courses and exchanging materials. This is extremely useful with LCTLs since there are often limited published materials, forcing instructors to create their own materials from scratch.

From students' perspectives, they can have access to a wider offering of languages and levels when no longer limited to the offerings from their home university. LCTL programs can be lonely, not only for the instructors that often work alone but also for students who are frequently in courses with small groups (even individual students, in some cases). BSL courses also allow students to meet, work, and create social bonds with other students interested in the same LCTL, something that can encourage active learning and enable them to become part of a learning community.

In addition to these LCTL-specific challenges, BSL offers advantages for teaching any language when compared to traditional online courses. Second language acquisition is strengthened by frequent interaction with the language, with more advanced speakers, and with a community of peers. Blended synchronous environments allow opportunities for more "face-to-face" interaction (even when that interaction is mediated through technology). Language learners also benefit from the ability to see the facial expressions and body language of their interlocutors, as well as the ability to receive feedback and ask questions spontaneously. This places added emphasis on the synchronous aspect of BSL and the importance and quality of its video conferencing, compared to some courses that rely more on asynchronous lectures and discussion.

In short, BSL can increase the visibility of LCTL programs, improve enrollments, and develop stronger and more stable language programs across universities. This has benefits that go beyond the students, instructors, and institutions involved in these courses, providing a stronger base for the teaching and learning of rarely taught languages in general.

Definitions

Many of the terms associated with online teaching and learning are used in slightly different ways by different researchers. The following definitions are intended to help readers understand how these terms are used in this book:

- *blended synchronous learning (BSL):* technology-mediated learning environments where face-to-face and remote students are joined synchronously.
- *face-to-face:* contexts where students and instructors are located in the same physical learning space.
- *remote students, online students:* students at remote locations who attend class through the use of technology, typically video conferencing.
- *video conferencing:* any use of audio and video to communicate over the internet. When specifying either traditional video conferencing technology (e.g., devices that use H.323 or SIP protocol) or software-based web conferencing applications, that distinction will be made clear.

2

Preparing BSL Environments

ALONG WITH THE benefits that BSL offers, it also brings many challenges that instructors, students, support staff, and administrators may have never encountered before. These environments multiply the number of learning spaces for a given course, with unique needs in each location. This section aims to highlight concerns that need to be addressed *before* beginning the process of creating BSL environments by outlining all the components necessary for both face-to-face and remote spaces, presenting recommendations for designing the physical layout of each space, comparing options for technology hardware and software, and discussing the training necessary for multiple roles of stakeholders. The end goal is to help those interested in implementing BSL do so as efficiently and effectively as possible.

Key Components of BSL Environments

Distributing learners across multiple environments in effect creates several puzzle boards, with some pieces that are needed in each and some that are unique to the different environments. Even those requirements that overlap often do not need to be identical in each location. The result is a range of options in terms of financial cost, quality, and ease of use, making BSL within reach for many institutions. This section begins with some elements that are needed in each environment, then looks at elements unique to the face-to-face classroom and to remote learning spaces.

Conferencing Equipment

One thing that makes BSL advantageous over more traditional online learning is the ability to create synchronous, social learning environments where all learners can see and hear each other. This is especially important for language learning, where communication and interaction are both pedagogical methods and the target objectives, and where instant feedback is essential. To enable this synchronous interaction, each location in BSL needs a camera, microphone, at least one monitor, speakers, some kind of device that ties it all together, and a reliable, high-speed internet connection. For a high-end classroom setup, this could mean tens of thousands of dollars' worth of specialized equipment installed into a semipermanent, conferencing-enabled learning space; for an individual attending a class remotely, all of this could be accomplished simply with a personal laptop computer. We will explore more options and recommendations in the following sections.

Before moving on, it should be noted that a second camera within a single location is a possibility in some situations. Additional cameras allow for more viewing angles that may lead to a more direct, face-to-face feeling between interlocutors. This can be beneficial or even necessary, especially in larger classrooms, if every student is to have the opportunity to speak into the camera from each seat. In a well-designed space there could be a number of presets that allow the camera to move directly to a given student or general area with the push of a single button, or even automatically if synchronized with a microphone. However, the small class sizes (both in number of students and size of the classroom) typical of LCTLs mean additional cameras are usually not necessary for teaching languages via BSL. Additional cameras also add an extra layer of complication to a BSL space and have the potential to increase demands on maintenance and the instructor's attention during class, making them more troublesome than beneficial in some cases.

Face-to-Face Classroom

Face-to-face classrooms in BSL environments are often hybrid spaces that combine some physical elements of more traditional classrooms with the technological components needed for video conferencing. The most essential carryovers from traditional classrooms are a writing surface and a screen for viewing content from the instructor's computer. For the writing surface, this might be a simple chalkboard or whiteboard; the challenge then becomes configuring the layout in such a way that the classroom's camera is able to include the instructor, students, and writing surface. This typically requires a camera with pan–tilt–zoom (PTZ) functionality, which can add to the cost but also improve the quality of interaction. Alternatively, BSL classrooms may use some kind of digital writing surface like a tablet or smartboard that can be shared directly with remote students via the conferencing application. This can make the content appear more clearly for all students, but using a tablet has the potential of making it more difficult for students to see details regarding *how* something is written, which can be valuable when working with unfamiliar scripts. Regarding monitors and projection screens, there are at least two things that typically need to appear on the screen: the instructor's computer content and the remote students. In some cases, these could appear on the same screen, though that means the screen "real estate" is limited for both. Two separate monitors allow both computer content and remote students to have adequate attention.

Another important note regards the use of audio and video materials in BSL environments. If the device that is playing the multimedia is different from the device that is running the meeting (a distinction that will be made clear in the following sections), extra care should be taken when setting up the learning space to ensure that the audio can be relayed directly to remote participants. In other words, when instructors share their screen they should be sharing audio as well. Otherwise, the audio remote students hear will be going out of the classroom speakers and into the classroom microphone, losing quality in the process. Maintaining the highest-quality sound possible is especially important in language classes, where students need to hear the nuances of pronunciation.

Remote Learning Spaces

Remote spaces typically have more flexibility simply because there is a wide range in where they occur and how many participants they need to accommodate. Some institutions strive to maintain a "classroom-to-classroom" relationship and require that remote students meet in an on-campus, conferencing-equipped classroom, and this does provide several benefits. First, this typically allows for better quality and reliability in equipment and connectivity, leading to a more stable connection, clearer communication, and less interruptions. Meeting in a campus classroom might also mean more access to technological support personnel, who can help start each meeting and troubleshoot any problems that arise. This can also put both groups, face-to-face and remote, on more equal footing since they are in similar physical environments, compared to individual students who may be joining from less formal spaces. But the benefits of these on-campus environments comes at the cost of a greater investment for institutions receiving courses by requiring dedicated spaces, equipment, and support staff, as well as the associated logistical challenges like room scheduling.

Remote BSL environments that have only one student at a given video endpoint offer the most flexibility as these students typically have the option of using all the necessary conferencing equipment within a single laptop computer. The student could attend from either a formal classroom, a semi-formal learning space that can be reserved in a library or language center, or in some cases their own dormitory or apartment. Here the connection, equipment, and environmental factors can vary and lead to problems for all learners if not managed properly, so it is important for instructors and technology staff to establish expectations before the course begins. While having remote students in a formal or semi-formal learning space is preferable, the ultimate motivation in BSL is making language courses available to students who otherwise would not have access. If a conferencing-equipped, on-campus learning space is not available, some ground rules can be established (for example, using a hardwired ethernet connection along with a headset and microphone) to in order to achieve the highest quality audio and video possible while connecting from a personal computer at home.

Choosing Technology

For many years, the high cost of video conference technology meant that conference rooms were often limited to corporate offices or other environments capable of managing the heavy financial investment. Software applications like Skype then emerged as a way to video conference for free using equipment that is typically built into personal devices. A middle ground has emerged, combining some elements of more traditional conferencing equipment with widely available web-based applications. This section discusses considerations, benefits, and drawbacks for each tier.

Traditional Video Conferencing Equipment

In this book we refer to "traditional video conferencing equipment" as hardware and associated software that is designed exclusively for video conferencing purposes. These are typically comprehensive proprietary systems created by companies such as Cisco and Polycom that include a camera, microphone, remote control or touch panel, and a codec device. This device unifies data from each element, encodes data for transmission, and decodes data received from remote participants via protocols such as H.323 or SIP. Each codec has its own IP address dedicated to the transmission of conferencing data, allowing for a direct connection between devices at various endpoints. The result of this specialized equipment is stable and secure video conferencing with the best audio and video quality available.

As one might expect, top-tier or "enterprise" quality video conferencing comes at a high cost and has some associated drawbacks. Traditional video conference units can cost anywhere from several thousand to tens of thousands of dollars to purchase, and the cost of installing and maintaining this equipment requires an initial investment that may be beyond the reach of some academic programs. With specialized equipment comes the need for specialized maintenance and troubleshooting, which can be costly in both financial terms and the amount of time required to set up maintenance appointments. Extra care and preparation is needed to avoid the nightmare scenario of technical difficulties at the start of a class with no sufficient troubleshooting expertise on site. Another limitation is that video conferencing units traditionally could only "talk" to other video conference units, meaning a single student in one location could not use a personal device to call into a video conference meeting. However, most providers now have software that allows users to join from personal devices (e.g., Cisco Webex, Polycom RealPresence), and third-party applications have emerged to fill this gap as well (e.g., Zoom, GoToMeeting). A final drawback with traditional video conferencing equipment is a lack of flexibility: these devices are designed to do one thing and do it very well, but they cannot be repurposed for other uses if there is a change in demand for BSL use or if the technology goes out-of-date.

Web Conferencing

An alternative to the heavy initial investment and lack of flexibility brought about by traditional video conferencing is web conferencing. Rather than using a specialized codec device, web conferencing uses a software application running on a personal computer or laptop as the "engine" for online meetings. Web conferencing is essentially similar to making a Skype or FaceTime call on your computer or mobile device, though there are a number of ways to improve quality and stability for reliable class-room use. With a collection of mid-level equipment in an on-campus learning space, web conferencing has the potential to provide a similar learning environment to traditional video conferencing systems at a frac-tion of the cost.

The first piece of equipment needed for a "do-it-yourself" web confer-encing setup is the computer that will be running the conferencing soft-ware. This may be a desktop computer installed in the classroom, or instructors could bring their own laptop. In the case of the latter, some long-term cable maintenance may be needed so that instructors can simply plug in their machine to get the meeting started with minimal equipment setup. A machine installed into the learning space would be preferable, and a hardwired ethernet connection is essential for a stable high-speed con-nection. When possible, the computer running the conferencing software should also be the computer the instructor uses when showing any presen-tations, videos, websites, or other materials on a projector or TV monitor; this allows the instructor to share the screen with remote students more easily than trying to call into the meeting on a separate device or attempt to have students view material via the camera.

Perhaps the most vital piece of specialized equipment for BSL in a class-room space, and therefore often the largest investment, is an external cam-era with PTZ capabilities. This ensures that remote students are able to view whichever classroom element is most essential at the time: the entire group of participants, a portion of the chalkboard or whiteboard, or other indi-vidual students. Most PTZ cameras come with a remote control enabling the instructor to quickly change the orientation of the camera as needed, as well as the ability to create presets that can switch the camera from, for example, the entire group to the chalkboard with the press of a button. A variety of external PTZ options are available across a range of prices, but take care in selecting a camera with the best combination of picture quality, field of view, and connection standard available within your budget.

The remaining pieces of equipment for BSL—microphones, speakers, and monitors—allow for the most flexibility. Conferencing microphones are designed to pick up sounds from participants spread out around a room. Low- to mid-range options should be serviceable for most small spaces, but spending more can allow for better quality, better range, and features that will remove extra noise. Echo cancellation is a necessity, but it should come standard on any device designed for conferencing purposes. External speakers may be needed in some instances, but the speakers that are built into either the TV monitor or the classroom should typically suffice. The first question regarding monitors is, how many? Two monitors are desirable in most cases so that computer content and remote participants can both be viewed at all times without fighting each other for on-screen real estate. The only drawback to having two monitors for web conferencing are the relatively minor annoyances that come from moving content between two screens. Once the instructor is comfortable putting remote students on one screen and content on the other this should not be a problem, but it is something to keep in mind for instructors who may be new to BSL or need extra training when using new technology.

It should be noted that the equipment listed here represents the minimum requirements for BSL environments. There are ample opportunities to add more equipment that can improve the quality of interaction for participants in each location, but each new piece of equipment also adds another element that requires attention and potential troubleshooting. It is up to the instructor and support staff to decide how much equipment is ideal for each context. It can be essential to have extra laptops or tablets on hand that students in the face-to-face classroom can use to connect with remote peers for pair work, or they could use their personal devices. The Models of BSL section later in this chapter explores more options for the integration of extra equipment.

Finally, when selecting equipment for a BSL environment keep in mind that some all-in-one web conferencing units are available that typically include a camera, microphone, speakers, remote control, and a device that unites these inputs and outputs into one computer connection. These are fine options, but they may not be as up-to-date as other individual pieces of equipment. Another all-in-one option is a simple laptop computer. Laptops are limited in terms of capabilities and quality and are typically not an ideal solution, but they can be useful for very small groups, very tight budgets, informal meetings, last-minute arrangements, and troubleshooting emergencies.

The most obvious benefit to using a do-it-yourself web conferencing setup is cost. For example, the University of Chicago Language Center recently purchased a traditional video conferencing unit and had it installed into a classroom, requiring an investment of approximately $15,000. In a different room, a Mac Mini, external PTZ camera, and table microphone were added to the existing TV monitor for an investment of $2,500. While these two projects were not identical in terms of classroom size or installation requirements, they do illustrate the wide difference in startup costs between the two options. Another benefit of web conferencing is that each piece of equipment—the computer, camera, and microphone—retains its individual value and can easily be repurposed, whereas a video conferencing codec runs greater risk of becoming obsolete. Web conferencing uses individual elements that instructors and support staff are more familiar with and therefore better able to troubleshoot on their own, rather than needing to call specialized audiovisual, networking, or conferencing technicians. A final benefit is that web conferencing applications allow users to join from a range of devices more easily than traditional video conferencing, which typically requires users to call from similar devices by default.

Designing BSL Spaces

Along with the decisions that come with choosing technology, it is important to think about how best to arrange the different elements within the learning space. The key component that will need to be considered is the location of the camera, monitor(s), chalkboard or whiteboard, face-to-face students, and instructor. The size of the classroom and the type of equipment used will likely factor into the decision. The primary motivations when designing the layout of the room should be ensuring that all students have full access to all elements of class content and participation, as well as reducing the cognitive load for the instructor as much as possible. Participants in all locations should be able to see and hear whichever elements of the class are most important at a given time; this may alternate between the instructor and the chalkboard, the instructor's voice and a presentation slideshow, and discussion with their peers. Meanwhile, instructors have to manage the equipment and students in multiple locations, along with more traditional classroom concerns. A well-designed learning environment can reduce the additional burden placed on instructors during class meetings, ideally limited to simply pressing a button to change the position of the camera or to share computer content with remote students.

One common layout for on-campus BSL spaces could be considered a "conference room" layout, similar to the configuration of some video conferencing spaces common in corporate settings: participants gathered around a conference table (or group of desks), facing remote participants who are often in a very similar environment at another location. The defining feature of this layout is both monitors (for content and participants) at the "front" of the room, typically side-by-side. The primary benefit of this layout is the fact that all participants are facing each other at all times, potentially creating the feeling that they are all sitting around the same table. Conversely, another common configuration could be described as a "lecture" layout: remote participants appear on a monitor on the back wall of the face-to-face classroom. This may be better for instructors who spend more time at the front of the classroom, since remote participants are blended in among face-to-face participants.

With either of these configurations, the one cardinal rule is to always have the camera as close to the monitor containing remote participants as possible, ideally directly above or directly below. This is vital for maintaining the feeling of face-to-face communication; otherwise, it is impossible to look at remote participants and the camera at the same time.

While both of these layouts have their benefits, the primary factor in deciding between the two is typically logistical, rather than pedagogical, and often comes down to the size of the classroom. Larger classrooms are more likely to have a large projection screen that covers much of the front wall of the room, making it impossible to add a second monitor. Smaller rooms may have more flexibility in adding two monitors side by side, which could prevent face-to-face students from having to turn around to speak to their remote peers and could lead to benefits in group dynamics.

Models of BSL

As mentioned throughout, BSL environments come in a variety of shapes and sizes. Along with the choice of technology and the design of the learning space, the number of remote students and the number of different endpoints (sites where remote students are located) play a factor in the layout of BSL environments. Figure 2.1 shows a range of models presented by Bell, Sawaya, and Cain (2014) that take into account these variables and have a resulting effect on the number of platforms used, the amount of

Figure 2.1. Synchromodal models topography summary (adapted from Bell, Sawaya, and Cain 2014).

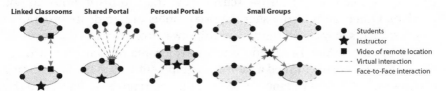

preparation and support needed for each meeting, and the overall feel of the interaction among participants at each location. This section will summarize each model and present advantages and disadvantages, while the article by Bell, Sawaya, and Cain provides more detailed descriptions, illustrations, and insights from their experiences in planning and designing, implementing, and adjusting each model.

Linked Classrooms

The linked classroom may be the simplest, most traditional form of BSL, where a group of students in one location connect to an instructor and group of students in another location. Linked classrooms are typically located in on-campus classrooms or learning spaces and most likely occur either at satellite campuses of a single institution, branch campuses of a state university system, or partner campuses within a cross-institutional collaboration. This model has more quality control and support than models where students attend individually, and the limited number of endpoints means less equipment in total and therefore less that can go wrong. There may also be pedagogical advantages to having multiple students in each location, particularly for language courses, so that students have easy access to pair and small group partners (though an overreliance on this convenient pairing may lead to a lack of diversity in interaction with other speakers). One potential drawback is that this model requires investment in equipment, space, and support at each location, and requiring such a space and group of classmates may limit access for some students.

Shared Portal

The shared portal model has several students from separate locations calling into class meetings and appearing on a single monitor (i.e., shared portal) within the the face-to-face classroom. For LCTL courses this may occur when there is only a single student attending from each remote campus or when remote students will be away from their home campus during some or all class meetings (e.g., if the schedules at the two institutions do not overlap). Other users of the shared portal model are graduate programs, where students may spend significant time away from campus due to work, family, or practicums. This model is relatively low maintenance for instructors because there is a limited amount of equipment within the face-to-face classroom, but it does put more responsibility on remote students, and the higher number of endpoints adds more potential for problems due to equipment malfunction, user error, or internet connectivity. As such, it is especially important to set ground rules and make sure students are properly trained, prepared, and supported. While there are applications that allow remote participants to join traditional video conference meetings from personal devices, the shared portal model may be better suited to web conferencing software that specializes in connecting from a variety of devices. Compared to the linked classroom model, each remote student is usually not a member of a remote cohort but instead is geographically isolated, so there is a particular need for instructors to utilize the strategies in chapter 3 of this book regarding group dynamics to make sure each student feels connected within the group.

Personal Portals

The personal portal model also has remote students at individual endpoints but has each student appear on a separate device within the face-to-face classroom, rather than collectively on a single screen. This model seeks to give all students a more similar presence and to "approximate more closely the experience of a traditional face-to-face large group setting" (Bell, Sawaya, and Cain 2014) by having remote students on tablets interspersed among face-to-face students. This can allow for a more natural feel in class discussion and group dynamics, to some degree, by giving each remote student their own space within the physical layout of the classroom. However, it must be noted that the personal portal model requires much more equipment, preparation, and support before and during each class meeting than the shared portal model. The tablets usually need to be set up before each meeting, both physically and in terms of connecting to the class meeting. During meetings, a face-to-face student may be assigned to help each remote student by being their eyes, ears, and voice within the classroom, making sure the tablet is pointing toward whoever is speaking. While this can help build relationships across physical boundaries, it also can have a detrimental effect on both groups: face-to-face students must divide their attention between their dual roles as student and technical support, and remote students become dependent upon face-to-face students being attentive to their needs. Also, having so many microphones and speakers within the face-to-face classroom can lead to serious audio problems. These problems may be alleviated by having technical support staff present within the face-to-face classrooms during class meetings, though this is unlikely to completely remove the extra strain on students' and instructors' attention and may be awkward in the low enrollments typical of LCTL classes. Ultimately, institutions implementing BSL will have to decide if there are enough benefits to the personal portal model to outweigh the considerable amount of resources (financial, human, and time) needed to implement it.

Small Groups

The small groups model is most appropriate for instructors and courses who place an emphasis on small group interaction during class meetings, which may make them a good model for language courses. This model has the physical layout of the face-to-face classroom divided into small groups consisting of both face-to-face and remote students. A balanced mixture would be ideal, but some groups may be entirely online or entirely face-to-face if there is a strong imbalance between the number of students in each location. This model has many of the same benefits and challenges of the personal portals model, but it has the added challenge of having multiple discussions occurring within the same physical space. This may require greater space between groups to limit audio interference or may even necessitate physical breakout rooms. It makes the virtual meeting space more complicated as well; it may require setting up multiple virtual meetings, which then requires careful preparation and communication regarding which students should be in which meeting space at which time. These problems are not limited to the small groups model but are present in any BSL setting where instructors strive for pair or small-group interaction that combines face-to-face and remote students. Some web conferencing applications allow for virtual breakout rooms which can make the process much simpler, and more insight on addressing these challenges can be found in Chapter 3.

This section has examined each model of BSL in isolation, but in reality BSL environments are likely to utilize multiple aspects of each model over time or even simultaneously. It is important for administrators, instructors, and support staff to analyze their goals and priorities for BSL settings through the lens of the available resources in order to find the environment that will provide the best possible experience for all students, then continue to evaluate and improve over time. The best model for each institution is likely not listed here but is yet to be created through persistent creativity, flexibility, and evaluation.

Training and Support

After the equipment has been selected and the learning space has been designed, it is important to provide adequate training to ensure that each class meeting runs as smoothly and efficiently as possible. This also ensures that the affordances of the equipment and software are best utilized, rather than simply meeting a minimum baseline of functionality. There are several groups that require training, and this training should begin far enough in advance that all parties know exactly what to expect on the first day of class.

Instructors

As the primary facilitator of class meetings, instructors carry a heavy load during BSL courses. On top of the lesson planning and classroom management that is ubiquitous among all courses, BSL instructors have the additional challenges of mediating technology and multiple groups of students. This is especially true for language courses, where clear communication and interaction among students is key. While working with unfamiliar technology may seem like the most daunting aspect of BSL, it is a relatively minor speed bump when compared to language pedagogy, group dynamics, and critical evaluation within this new setting. It is easier to train instructors on the use of new technology than it is train them on the creativity and flexibility needed for utilizing it effectively for language teaching. Chapter 3 discusses these challenging issues, while this section focuses on technical training.

The three main things instructors must be very familiar with well before the first day of class are the basic use of the conferencing technology (hardware and software), basic troubleshooting, and general knowledge of the more advanced features and possibilities within the BSL environment. Understanding the basics of using the equipment (e.g., starting and ending meetings, adjusting the camera and volume, muting the microphone, sharing computer content) helps maintain instructor independence and autonomy; while it may be helpful for support staff to help start meetings, prolonged help may cause instructors to be dependent on support and incapable of starting meetings on their own when support is not available. Familiarization with the basic technology should start well in advance of the course start date and should include a series of training sessions that move from more hands-on to almost completely hands off, so that instructors are able to demonstrate and answer questions about the basic use of technology before class begins. This training should include both live tutorials and written reference materials.

Knowledge of basic troubleshooting is another factor that not only maintains an instructor's independence but is vital for maintaining efficient and effective time management during class meetings. Waiting for support staff to arrive and solve problems can kill the flow of a class and waste valuable time (as well as being awkward and embarrassing). Of course there may be times where unforeseen technical issues arise and technical assistance is unavoidable, but well-trained instructors should be aware of the first line of defense against common issues that might be expected. This is true for both the face-to-face classroom and for remote environments. Technical issues at one endpoint can kill the productivity of all students; instructors should be familiar enough with the technology used at each endpoint to make an educated guess on the problem and offer some possible solutions. If those fail they can then call for external support, either on-site or at the remote location. Troubleshooting training can be performed in concert with training on the basic use of equipment, and reference materials can be printed and posted within the BSL space.

The third aspect, advanced features and options (i.e., any functionalities that are possible within the BSL environment but are not immediately necessary for class meetings), may actually have the need of coming first in the training process. Instructors will not have concrete need of using the technology before the class starts, but they must know what affordances are possible so they can properly plan activities and protocols that will best utilize the available technology for their learning goals and teaching style. Examples of this may be breakout rooms or whiteboard tools within the conferencing software or how to integrate external applications or equipment effectively (e.g., using a word processing application to demonstrate how a word is spelled rather than switching from screen sharing to the chalkboard or using personal devices to facilitate pair work). This is another area where technological affordances must be combined with creativity, flexibility, and language pedagogy knowledge.

Finally, instructors and support staff can decide together the ground rules that all students are expected to follow. Some may be more applicable to either face-to-face or remote students, and some may be focused more on either time management or group dynamics. For example, remote students may be required to be "present" at class meetings at least five minutes before the meeting starts to ensure that all equipment is functioning properly before class begins. Meanwhile, face-to-face students may need to be told that they are expected to attend all class meetings in person and do not have the option of attending online (though some flexibility may be beneficial in cases where students would otherwise miss a class meeting).

Students

Students are another group that must be familiar with the basic use and troubleshooting of conferencing technology, though the different groups of students have different responsibilities. Remote students need to receive training on use and troubleshooting similar to that of instructors, but they should also be reminded that their ability to meet expectations and follow rules has a significant effect on the experience of all their classmates. Minor sounds or disturbances at one endpoint will be amplified through the speakers and headphones at all others. Ground rules are especially important for remote students attending class independently and may include

- using a wired broadband connection or wireless connection that exceeds the requirements set by the conferencing software selected,
- using a space that will be quiet and free from distraction or interruption for the duration of the meeting,
- dressing as you would for any other class,
- not eating during class meetings and being mindful of other noises (including typing and writing),
- using a headset with a microphone,
- muting your microphone when not speaking, in case unforeseen noises arise, and
- knowing what to do in the event of technical difficulties.

Face-to-face students have less explicit requirements for training, but they should also be aware of how extraneous sound within the face-to-face classroom is amplified at other endpoints. Knowledge of the basic use and troubleshooting of equipment can also be beneficial for these students, as they may be able to help the instructor at times, though they should not be expected to provide so much attention to technology mediation that it interferes with their attention to class content. In the authors' experience, both groups of students are usually flexible, patient, and highly motivated when studying languages in BSL settings: remote students because they are appreciative of the opportunity to study a language that they could not otherwise access, and face-to-face students because they have a unique opportunity to interact with students at other locations. However, both groups may lose patience if they feel that the learning space, instructor, or support staff is not adequately prepared.

Support Staff

Integral to the training of students and instructors is the work of the technical support staff who will be designing and conducting the training. They will need to have comprehensive knowledge of the equipment and software, need to be able to transfer that knowledge effectively, and should be able to think ahead to all of the different challenges that might be expected. Representatives from these departments should be involved at the technology-selection stage, both as a resource to provide expertise in the decision but also so they feel more invested in helping make sure it works effectively. There can be a large difference in the expertise needed between web conferencing and traditional video conferencing, so technical support for BSL environments may come from language center or general campus IT staff or may require specialists from networking or video communications departments, which can incur extra costs.

Some previous research (e.g., Bell, Cain, and Sawaya 2013) has recommended a "technology navigator," or a technology support person who is on hand within the face-to-face classroom. This helps disperse some of the cognitive load away from the instructor and would eliminate the need for instructors to waste valuable class time waiting for technology support, and it becomes more valuable with more participants, remote endpoints, and equipment in the classroom. However, for LCTL classes with very low enrollments and an emphasis on interpersonal communication, it should suffice to design the learning space to be as accessible as possible, make sure instructors and students receive proper training, and have support staff available close enough for only minimal disruption, rather than having a staff member sit in on all class meetings. This could be a great role for graduate assistants, though language courses with small enrollments may not have graduate assistants.

Cross-institutional Challenges

An entire new set of challenges is added when BSL courses are part of cross-institutional partnerships. Often referred to as "course sharing," these partnerships allow students from one institution to enroll in courses at another and are particularly useful for specialized subjects like LCTLs, where some languages may be taught at only a few universities across a country. In other cases, member universities of a regional consortium may use course sharing as a way to offer students access to a more diverse array of language courses than one single university can provide. This section explores some of the challenges introduced when students within a single BSL course come from different universities.

The first requirement needed for cross-institutional course sharing is some kind of formal partnership that serves as the mechanism to enable such collaboration. This often comes in the form of a memorandum of understanding established by upper-level administrators that sets the policy guidelines for course-sharing procedures. For example, the University of Chicago is a member of CourseShare, a program within the Big Ten Academic Alliance. CourseShare's memorandum of understanding allows students to enroll in and receive credit for courses at other member institutions without paying any extra tuition. As such, these course-sharing partnerships require administrators that see the value such exchanges can offer their students and their academic programs, even when these exchanges may go against the bottom line. With the volatility that can surround fragile language programs and the instructors who teach them, members of partner institutions must be able to commit to continuing to offer a given language for a specified amount of time before entering into a partnership.

There are numerous logistical challenges that come from adding students from another university into a course. One is scheduling: some universities still operate on the quarter system, and even universities that have generally similar calendars rarely have identical start dates, end dates, and university holidays. Differing time zones can also be a factor that can lead to confusion. As a general rule, the university offering the course sets the schedule, and students from other universities are expected to adhere to the host institution's academic calendar. Another problem can be granting students access to learning management systems or other necessary platforms. Again, it is typically the host university's responsibility to ensure that all students can access all components of the course. Logistical nightmares can arise simply from the number of administrative staff members involved in making shared courses happen. Enrollment, technical support, and room scheduling are all factors that may require attention from separate individuals at each participating institution, as well as language instructors, department chairs, and academic advisors. It is essential that each institution establish clear protocols and communication and that partners are established well in advance of a course's start date, ideally at least one full semester before.

Related to the amount of work that goes into each shared-course partnership is the issue of promoting and attracting students to these courses, which can be a double-edged sword. Shared courses can expand a university's course offerings, but they are not a sustainable way to meet the needs of every individual student. Universities entering course-sharing partnerships need strategic ways of identifying language needs, both for their students and for programs that need expanded enrollment, so that administrative and support staff are not stretched thin by an overwhelming number of requests. The challenge then becomes communicating the opportunities that shared courses can provide, but only within a limited audience. The solution that the CourseShare program uses is for partnerships to be initiated and agreed upon by departments at each institution, not by individual students. These departments should identify languages that their students would benefit from accessing. Campus coordinators then help find partner institutions to set up exchanges that can ideally be in place for multiple years, minimizing the amount of administrative labor needed and making course sharing more sustainable.

Conclusion

Chapter 2 of this book has attempted to highlight the many issues that institutions will need to think about before embarking on the exciting challenge of BSL courses, but undoubtedly many more unforeseen challenges will arise. While it is impossible to plan for all of them specifically, it is absolutely vital to plan for them generally. Flexibility and creativity are necessary components when preparing BSL environments, and they will become even more important when exploring language teaching pedagogy in chapter 3.

Tips and Recommendations

- Traditional video conferencing devices can offer better quality but are more expensive and require more support. Web conferencing is more affordable and more flexible, but may require a tradeoff in audio-video quality.

- While extra equipment can lead to a more personal experience, it also requires more attention and presents more opportunities for things to go wrong.
- A camera with PTZ functionality and programmable presets is essential for the face-to-face classroom.
- Make sure the camera is positioned either directly above or below the monitor where participants appear.
- Set guidelines for expectations of remote students, especially if they are attending from an off-campus location.
- Make sure instructors receive adequate training to perform basic use and troubleshooting of equipment well before the first day of class.
- Cross-institutional partnerships can require a great deal of administrative resources. Be sure to establish clear protocols and set up arrangements months in advance.

3

Pedagogical Challenges

ON THE SURFACE, BSL courses may appear to be environments where online students simply attend a traditional face-to-face course remotely in which, as long as technology works properly (e.g., strong connection, clear picture), few further changes might arise. We define BSL, however, as technology-mediated learning environments where face-to-face and remote students are joined synchronously, so in BSL courses, both face-to-face and remote students interact in a *new environment*. When designing a BSL course, instructors are not creating a face-to-face course that will be open to remote students; they are designing a course in a new setting with two (or more) separate groups of students in mind.

Blended synchronous learning changes a course from top to bottom: its design, methods of delivery, group dynamics, activities, the way instructors provide input and feedback, and all other aspects of the course. It is very important to keep that in mind, from the first steps of course design to final assessments.

Ideally, these two groups (face-to-face and remote students) would be fully blended into one group, creating a seamless environment regardless of location (see figure 3.1). But realistically the result is very often two groups that share one common space—hopefully for a period of time as long as possible—but that at times are in separate, different spaces (see figure 3.2). That means that each group has different needs and that instructors have to adapt their course for each group, including input, feedback, and delivery method.

30

Figure 3.1. Idealistic blending of face-to-face and distance students.

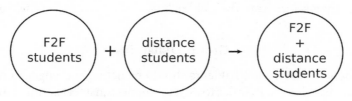

The goal is for the overlapping space to be as large as possible, with activities that facilitate seamless interaction. At the same time, BSL courses should take advantage of this shared space—using it wisely, with cooperative and active learning activities. That means that instructors keep doing two processes back and forth: designing activities and settings that promote interaction among students and at the same time making sure that they use that space for active and cooperative learning. In the case of language learning, this the perfect space for communicative activities.

With the goal of two groups merged in one environment that combines a common space as wide as possible, some pedagogical challenges arise, including how to

- build positive group dynamics among all students,
- facilitate cooperative and active learning,
- find the best methods of delivery, and
- provide appropriate feedback.

When looking for solutions to those challenges, instructors, staff, and also students will be able to rely on their knowledge of how a class works. But,

Figure 3.2. Realistic blending of face-to-face and distance students.

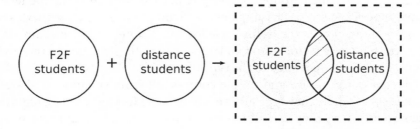

at the same time, they will often have to think outside the box, be creative, separate themselves from their old habits, and imagine new solutions.

Group Dynamics

In a language classroom, students should be active and engaged in communicative activities. In order to do so students must feel comfortable with their peers, making positive group dynamics indispensable. Group dynamics can be challenging in any class with only one environment (face-to-face or online), but in BSL, where face-to-face and remote students are combined, the challenge is even greater.

In *Group Dynamics in the Language Classroom* (2003), Dörnyei and Murphey warn about the challenges of split groups: "communicative teaching activities often require *small group work* and active *interaction* among the students, which would be very difficult to achieve if, say, the class was split up into cliques who did not communicate with each other." BSL environments do not imply the presence of cliques, but they do imply a certain level of separation between face-to-face and remote students. Building bridges or blurring the borders between those groups of students is key for successful group dynamics in BSL environments.

While becoming part of a new group in a face-to-face class is usually something familiar for both students and teachers, dealing with group dynamics in a BSL classroom can be a new experience for everyone involved. Therefore, it will often be necessary not only to implement traditional group building techniques but also to be creative about learning and using new ones adapted to BSL needs.

The first step in forming positive group dynamics is actually becoming a group. Dörnyei and Malderez (1997) gather a list of factors that can enhance group affiliation: proximity, contact, interaction, and cooperation between members for common goals; successful completion of whole group tasks and a sense of group achievement; intergroup competition (e.g., games in which groups compete); joint hardship that group members have experienced (e.g., carrying out a difficult physical task together); and common threat (e.g., the feeling of fellowship before a difficult exam). We can classify these factors into two larger groups: those related to the environment and those related to the type of activities.

In both face-to-face and online courses, all enrolled students share a single space where they typically are all on equal footing: either a physical classroom where they can all interact in person or a virtual space like a learning management system (LMS) where they are all online. The challenge in both is to unite those students into one single group. In a BSL course there is an extra challenge, as we have already seen, due to a physical barrier between face-to-face and remote students. Here instructors have to not only unite those individual students into their respective groups but also constantly strive to reduce the barrier between these two groups, creating activities that promote interaction among all students.

Since the physical barriers between online and face-to-face students cannot be completely removed, interaction among all participants is a primary goal for BSL instructors seeking to develop positive group dynamics. Going back to figure 3.2, it is key to focus on widening and taking advantage of the overlapping space as much as possible. This requires a concentrated effort to foster interactions between the instructor and all students and among all students themselves, both inside and outside the classroom.

Interaction outside of the Classroom

Sometimes the first instinct is to think that the shared space of interaction between face-to-face and remote students is limited to the time spent in the classroom working in pair or group activities. That is what often happens in a traditional face-to-face class, where very often the time spent in class is dedicated to communicative activities in groups, while work outside the classroom tends to be done individually.

In BSL environments, classroom time is invaluable but often insufficient to overcome the added barriers between face-to-face and online students. Therefore, instructors can take better advantage of students' time outside the classroom by using online resources to improve group dynamics. Online environments have a significant advantage in BSL: when interacting online outside the classroom, all students are in the same environment, and the face-to-face/online dichotomy disappears.

In addition to being a way to simply organize materials and assignments, an online platform that centralizes course content (e.g., an LMS, blog, or wiki) is an excellent first step in merging all members of the course into one group, creating an online agora where students can access content but also gather, communicate, and learn together. While the barrier between face-to-face and remote students will always be present during class meetings, creating a virtual learning space by integrating multiple online tools into a single online setting allows for a truly blended environment outside the classroom.

Traditionally, LMSs are often used unidirectionally as an information board where instructors post materials, individual activities, and information that students access from their personal devices (with the exception of the occasional discussion board). Advancements in multimedia, conferencing, and mobile technologies allow instructors to design a wide range of online communicative activities, which can be a great asset for BSL courses. As a result, when designing a BSL course instructors can think about moving part of the interaction from inside the classroom to online environments with activities and tools that facilitate interaction among peers, both synchronous and asynchronous: discussion boards (with written, audio, or audiovisual texts), collaborative writing tools, online survey tools, and video conferencing software.

The time outside the classroom is very useful for interactions both among students and also between the instructor and students. According to Popov (2009, 6), in BSL environments "distance students often expressed disappointment that they did not have the possibility of interacting with the teachers while they were lecturing and also immediately after a lecture." LCTL classrooms tend to have small enrollments, making it easy for instructors and students to find one-on-one moments in face-to-face classrooms in the form of a brief conversation at the end of the class, asking a few questions between activities, or a side question while working in groups. In BSL those moments are rare; video conferencing with the whole group (as is the case in BSL) makes one-on-one private moments more difficult for face-to-face students and almost impossible for remote students, but those interactions are indispensable. They provide an opportunity to ask and answer questions, give feedback and extra input, and get to know each other better. Once again, online software allows instructors to create useful one-on-one moments and equal opportunities for all students through online office hours, online individual or group homework consultation, and written and oral feedback. Rethinking online interaction outside of the classroom time through these and other creative methods can open the door to numerous opportunities for interaction among all participants of a course.

Interaction inside of the Classroom

The interaction inside BSL classrooms is typically synchronous, making the time more defined, structured, and limited. Because of that, in a communicative and student-centered course the role of the instructor—comparable to that of an orchestra conductor—is vital. In BSL the instructor is key when promoting interaction among all learners, but especially between face-to-face and remote students.

Inside the classroom there are different kinds of interaction. When the interaction is mainly between the instructor and individual students (e.g., asking questions to the whole group or individuals), it is very useful for the instructor to move back and forth from face-to-face to remote students, making sure that students from both environments are included in the activity and, therefore, avoiding a feeling of disconnection. Previous research shows that the instructor not paying enough attention to one of the groups is one of the main concerns of students participating in BSL courses (Popov 2009; Rogers et al. 2003), and conscious, balanced interaction with all students by switching alternatively between face-to-face and remote students is a good strategy to keep all students equally engaged.

When interaction happens among all students, both with the whole class or in smaller groups, the role of the instructor is also crucial in making sure that face-to-face and remote students interact with each other from the very beginning of the course. The first classes spent together are of vital importance to the future functioning of the group (Dörnyei and Malderez 1997), so creating positive interaction habits from the beginning will help with the group dynamics for the rest of the course. The instructor can establish certain norms or habits in the first class meetings that students will mimic in the future.

Some examples of in-class activities that can help foster relationships between all students are listed below:

- Large-group activities, like chain games, where each part of the chain switches from a face-to-face student to a remote student then back to a face-to-face student. The information can be question and answer, where one student asks a question, the other answers and asks another question to a different student (e.g., Student 1: *What's your name?* Student 2: *My name is . . . and you, what's your name?* Student 3: *My name is . . . and you . . .*). It could also be accumulative, with a list of vocabulary where each student adds a word (e.g., Student 1: *In the basket there is an apple.* Student 2: *In the basket there is an apple and two cookies . . .*) or a story where each student adds a sentence (e.g., Student 1: *Once upon a time, there was a small town surrounded by mountains.* Student 2: *Once upon a time, there was a*

small town surrounded by mountain. The inhabitants of that town had a big problem . . .).
- Subgroup activities where face-to-face students and remote students are mixed and interact through video conference software on personal computers or tablets. In that case, adding a written communicative tool (chat, collaborative writing tool) can be very useful, so students can communicate both orally and through writing.

These examples should not imply that all activities happening inside the classroom must engage face-to-face and remote students together. Sometimes it might be more convenient (because of the activity, the software, the time, or just to make things easier for students) to have face-to-face and remote students work separately. What is important is to identify what activities work better in what type of groups and find a balance between all of them. While face-to-face settings have a natural advantage in regard to fostering group dynamics, BSL environments can be made more equitable through activities like these that seek to place all students in frequent contact with their peers and on an even playing field, regardless of their physical location.

Delivery Method

In BSL environments it is especially important to "expect the unexpected," as said in any teacher training course, and teaching, proaction, and preparation are key for a successful class and course. When thinking about input and delivery method, being proactive, preparing in advance, and having students prepare in advance avoids complications during class time.

Because of the dual settings of BSL environments, providing input inside the classroom can be more challenging than in a traditional classroom or an online course, especially for remote students. Even with excellent audio and video technology, remote students may miss part of what is happening in class; they often have only a partial view of the classroom, they may miss instructor or peer gestures, or small audio issues may occur. Because of that, providing them with the input multiple times, in different formats, and via various channels improves the opportunities for all students to have equal access to that input.

Giving students the chance to look at content in advance allows them to come to class prepared. Then, the input that the instructor provides inside the class builds on what they have already learned by themselves. That makes understanding the class content and dealing with any possible technology challenges easier. Flipped content is an excellent way of accomplishing this. Providing students with the content of grammar and vocabulary that will be used in class—or part of it—benefits both remote and face-to-face students, who can work on that content in advance and at their own pace. Flipped content also frees class time to be dedicated to communicative activities. If any technological problems arise during a BSL class meeting, it is easier to deploy student-centered communicative activities while the instructor troubleshoots if students already know the content for the lesson.

Other than flipped content that students work with mainly before class, the instructor can give other revision materials (e.g., handouts and videos) that students can check after class. Both materials allow students to learn autonomously and solve part of the questions by themselves, and having that material available releases them from the in-class stress of "if I miss something now, it will be missed forever."

Providing students with input in different formats before and after the classroom benefits all students in the course, both face-to-face and online ones. But there are other tips that focus especially on remote students. Despite working with the most reliable technological tools, sometimes the connection breaks, the audio does not work, or other problems arise. Even if those issues happen very rarely, these situations disrupt the class and create stress for everybody: remote students because they cannot follow what is happening in the classroom, face-to-face students because the flow of the classroom has been interrupted, and the instructor, who is trying to fix the problem while accommodating all students.

Tips to deal with those situations will be discussed later in this book, but a helpful trick is to have backup activities that students can do while the problem is being fixed. In addition, it is useful to provide remote students with a schematic lesson plan that allows them to follow the pace of the classroom and continue partly on their own when technological issues arise. When remote students have schematic lesson plans, it also makes it easier for the teacher to give instructions (e.g., "look for document X," "open file Y").

Finally, as previously said, it is challenging to find one-on-one moments with remote students in class. Therefore, facilitating one-on-one moments outside the classroom—where students can ask questions and receive feedback and also, when necessary, where instructors can provide input on some topics covered in the class (revision, further explanations)—can be extremely helpful when designing input delivery methods.

Feedback

Of all the advantages that BSL offers for remote students over traditional online courses, the possibility of receiving individual feedback, along with interaction, might be the most relevant for language learning. Interaction and feedback are key when learning a foreign language, and data shows that those are subjects of concern for remote students participating in BSL courses, especially when they experience a lack of or a delay in the teacher's feedback (Popov 2009).

Taking into consideration its form, we can make distinctions between synchronous and asynchronous feedback, individual and group feedback, and written and oral feedback; we can also establish a progression between automatic and personalized feedback.

Automatic Feedback

Traditionally, automatic feedback often came in the form of an answer key for a set of exercises. Students would do some exercises and then have access to the solutions at the end of the book or in a separate booklet. Many books still offer that option, but we also now have technological tools that allow students to do activities online and get a correction and some sort of feedback: the accuracy of the response, the correct answer, or even a comment or a link to an explanation.

This feedback has its advantages: it releases correction and feedback from in-class time, and it gives autonomy to students to do exercises at their own pace or go back and forth between their answers and the correction, and it can provide exercises for their specific level (i.e., some students can work reviewing previous content and others can move forward or work with more challenging exercises). This feedback is also synchronous, as students don't have to wait to know the right answer.

This kind of automatic feedback is common in digital or online platforms and can often be found in exercises on LMSs that are part of a traditional or online language course or online workbooks, self-taught courses, or massive open online courses (MOOCs). While still useful, this feedback is very limited and not personalized to the learner's strengths and weaknesses.

Personalized Written Feedback

Because personalized written feedback is usually asynchronous and produced outside of the classroom, it is very easy to integrate in BSL environments.

Not only is it easy to integrate, but in BSL environments its uses can be expanded. While in face-to-face classes written feedback might be limited to compositions and other assignments, in BSL courses it can become a stronger way for the instructor to communicate with students and provide a wider range of feedback—not only assignment feedback (like comments using track-changes tools, short paragraphs at the end of a task) but also periodical, formative feedback (either weekly or biweekly, messages with comments of students' global performance, tips, or links).

In face-to-face classrooms group feedback is usually oral, synchronous, and in-class, but in BSL environments it is beneficial to explore written feedback as a tool for providing group feedback. Asynchronous written feedback (e.g., an email or message to the whole class) blurs the border between face-to-face and remote students. Since all students are in the same online environment, the instructor can be sure that the feedback has been delivered to all students in an equal manner and can also ensure that students have access to the feedback whenever they need it. They can go back to it on their own, which can be very useful when feedback contains long explanations or links to relevant information. Written group feedback does not have to replace oral feedback in class; it can complement it.

Personalized Asynchronous Oral Feedback

Traditionally most oral feedback has been synchronous, but the proliferation of recording technology and personal devices allows instructors to move part of the traditional written feedback to asynchronous oral feedback. LMSs often provide an audio/video recording feature, but instructors have other recording software available (from simple recording software accessible on their phones, tablets or computers to more elaborate hardware and software that their universities can typically provide).

This kind of software might involve a small learning curve for instructors and students, but once the users are used to it, it has several advantages:

- It can save in-class time for other activities.
- Once used to the technology, recording is fast; instructors can provide more detailed feedback in less time, with longer explanations and more examples.
- It allows instructors to give private and personalized feedback on oral skills, something extremely important when learning a foreign language. This traditionally happens in class, in front of the whole group.
- Students can access this valuable feedback as often as they would like.

Instructors can record short audio clips to give students feedback on an oral activity (e.g., students' recording an audio clip about a subject, an oral activity done in class) and also to provide further feedback on written activities (e.g., reading aloud a task written by a student so the student can hear how the text sounds in the foreign language and improve pronunciation). Oral feedback (with the instructor's voice, tone, and even video image) can feel more personalized to students and can improve their sense of connection to the instructor and the group, something especially important for remote students. Most of the examples so far are of individual feedback, but this kind of feedback can also be used for whole-group feedback: for example, giving feedback after a group activity, like a debate; pointing out errors or giving tips to improve their speaking skills; wrapping-up that week's content with a weekly message to the whole group; and providing some tips, extra material, or follow-up activities.

Asynchronous oral feedback is an example of how BSL can encourage creativity and exploration of new resources that traditionally are not present in face-to-face environments.

Synchronous Oral Feedback

Oral synchronous feedback is probably the kind of feedback that traditionally people would think about when talking about "oral feedback": feedback given to the whole group in class after an activity, individual feedback given in class, or feedback given one-on-one during office hours.

This feedback is still extremely valuable in BSL environments, but it is important to take into consideration that sometimes this feedback might have some limitations and may not be the best for remote students. Even with excellent technology tools, remote students might miss part of what is happening in class; also, oral synchronous feedback often takes the form of one-on-one interaction and it is very difficult, if not impossible, to find in-class, one-on-one moments with remote students. To balance out this lack of individualized oral feedback, instructors can do two things: integrate other forms of feedback, as previously discussed (i.e., written feedback and asynchronous oral feedback), and find one-on-one moments outside the classroom to provide synchronous oral feedback (e.g., online office hours or online homework consultation).

As stated previously, a lack of or delay with the teacher's feedback is one of the primary concerns of remote students taking part in BSL courses

(Popov 2009), and synchronous oral feedback might be the kind of feedback that makes students feel the most connected within a course. Therefore, it is crucial to find ways to integrate it into BSL environments.

Exploring and testing all these different kinds of feedback (written, oral, group, individual, synchronous, asynchronous) can benefit not only BSL students—especially remote students—but can allow instructors and students to discover new ways of providing and receiving feedback more appropriate for specific needs. When designing a BSL course it is important to keep all of them in mind, see what works best in the given context, and use the most appropriate form of feedback in each situation.

Activities

For someone observing a BSL course, the classroom setting is the first difference they would notice. The next thing that would stand out is the unique design to the activities. The pedagogical principles of the previous sections provide the foundation of a BSL course, and designing activities built on top of that foundation requires creativity from instructors. Activities should

- promote interaction among all students and improve group dynamics;
- take advantage of online tools where all students are "online students," all in the same environment;
- be proactive, make sure that students come prepared and have had access to the input in advance (i.e., flipping content);
- encourage students to practice all four skills (speaking, reading, listening, and writing) outside of the classroom, and make special attention to move or add speaking tasks outside of the class meeting times;
- ensure individual feedback—as much as possible given the limitations of the setting; and
- promote activities that provide private spaces for individual feedback (such as online homework consultation or online assignments with written/oral feedback).

Extended Activities that Promote Interaction among All Students

One way to design successful activities for BSL environments is to split them into multiple parts. In doing so, students are engaged throughout the process of doing an assignment at home, following up on assignments completed by or with their peers, and performing a wrap-up assignment based on the work of their classmates. Each segment can incorporate different online tools. When split into an at-home, follow-up, and a wrap-up section, each activity can challenge a student in multiple communicative skills.

Adapting Activities for BSL Environments

A key skill for BSL instructors is the ability to adapt familiar, proven language-learning activities into these challenging new environments spread out over time and space. This includes having a repertoire of online tools that can serve multiple purposes. The use of collaborative tools when adapting traditional activities can improve group dynamics and student interaction among face-to-face and remote students. It also allows remote students to get synchronous (or asynchronous) personalized feedback from the instructor.

When dividing students into pairs/groups, the instructor can include both remote and face-to-face students in each pair or group, and/or pair or group remote students together and face-to-face students together. The first option may help with group dynamics, but it can involve additional technical challenges. It typically requires the use of extra devices (e.g., laptops, tablets, or phones) and applications. Making it possible will depend on the specific layout and equipment of the BSL setup, as outlined in chapter 2. It is up to the instructor to assess the situation of the class and make the best arrangements. In any case, it is recommended that students know how they will be paired in advance in order to save in-class time, avoid confusion, and allow more time for instructions; students should be able to focus on the instructions of the activity, not the instructions on how to split into groups.

The following table presents a number of examples of how activities that will be familiar to most language classrooms can be adapted for BSL environments. Language teachers are encouraged to use these examples as inspiration to find innovative ways of delivering their favorite activities in this challenging but exciting setting.

Tips and Recommendations

The following is a list of smart tricks that aim to reduce the possible issues that can happen often in BSL, reduce the consequences of those problems,

Table 3.1. At-home, follow-up, and wrap-up assignments

	Part 1: Individual at-home assignment	Part 2: Peer follow-up	Part 3: Wrap-up task
Describing yourself	Video recording: students describe themselves (1 min. max). *Speaking.*	Students watch their peers' videos at home. *Listening.*	Students write sentences describing their peers. *Writing.*
Describing and guessing famous people	Video recording: Students describe a famous person without revealing the name. *Speaking.*	Students watch their peers' videos at home. *Listening.*	Students guess the names of the famous people and provide their answers using a polling software tool (e.g., Google Forms).
Presenting and discussing personal topics	Video recording: students talk about a subject (holidays, their favorite dish, favorite movie) (1 min. max). *Speaking.*	Students watch their peers' videos at home. *Listening.*	Option 1. Students write a summary protocol. *Writing.* Option 2. Students write questions to ask to their peers, as a reply. *Writing.* Option 3. Students bring questions to class for their peers and discuss the content in class. *Speaking.*
Blogs and wikis	Students create a blog/wiki and they add articles periodically. *Writing.*	Students read their peers' posts and think of questions to ask. *Reading.*	Option 1. Students write questions in the comments section to ask to their peers, as a reply. The author of the blog/wiki answers them. *Writing.* Option 2. Students bring questions to class for their peers and discuss the content in class. *Speaking.*
Online oral presentation	Video recording: Students record a presentation about a subject (using PowerPoint or a similar program and screen recording software). *Speaking.*	Students watch their peers' videos at home. *Listening.*	Students bring questions to class for their peers and discuss the content in class. *Speaking.*
Online written presentations	Students write a short text (one or two paragraphs) about a subject (description, narration, present a piece of news, etc.). *Writing.*	Students read their peers' texts at home. *Reading.*	Option 1. Using a "forum," create a discussion on that subject. *Writing.* Option 2. Students bring questions to class and discuss them. *Speaking.*

Table 3.2. Adapting traditional activities to BSL environments

	Brief description in face-to-face environments	*Adapting for BSL environments*	*Notes*
Vocabulary game: writing lists	In groups, students write a list of vocabulary on a specific subject (e.g., professions, food, etc.), then share them with the rest of the class.	Use a collaborative tool where all students have access to the same document (e.g., Padlet). Students write a list of vocabulary on a specific subject. Since they have access to their peers' work, students cannot repeat words that have been used by other groups.	Since students cannot repeat words from other groups, this activity is more challenging than the traditional one. At the end of the activity students have access to the complete list of vocabulary; this list can become a study tool.
In class review: listing and summarizing content	Individually or in groups, students list content (e.g., questions/answers of a job interview; questions/answers in a restaurant). The content is put together orally and the instructor writes it on the board. Students copy it.	Using collaborative tools where all students have access to the same document (e.g., Padlet), students brainstorm the linguistic content. After that, the whole class goes through it, and the instructor makes the appropriate corrections. As a result, students end up with a handout made collectively.	This activity saves in-class time, since there is no need to copy the sentences several times. Students work on a communal document that compiles a review of the subject and is a product of group work.
Pair work	Students work autonomously in pairs or small groups, practicing communicative situations, working on a text, etc. The instructor walks around the room, answering questions and providing feedback.	Create "breakout rooms" for pair work using video conference software. The instructor can access these breakout rooms in order to observe, answer questions, or provide feedback.	Students have to know in advance who they will be paired with, what software will be used, and how to use it. Students can be encouraged to use audio and also the chat option to write down vocabulary, record specific information, use it as a notepad, etc.
Pair work II	In class, students interview each other about a subject (routine, hobbies, holidays, etc.), and they report on the information they have gathered.	Students gather outside the classroom to do pair work (in person or online) and they write a text reporting the information they have gathered.	This way of organizing pair work makes it easy to pair remote and face-to-face students together.

In-class writing	Students in groups write a dialogue, short paragraph, etc. (usually as a follow-up or wrap-up activity).	Using a writing collaborative tool (e.g., Google Docs, EtherPad), students write a dialogue or text in groups. After that, they can share it with the class (usually orally but also in the written form).	When dividing the students in groups: Option 1. Remote and face-to-face students work in separate groups (remote students together and face-to-face students together). The instructor has access to the document and provides feedback. Option 2. Remote and face-to-face students are paired together and use the chat function to communicate. Instructor has access to the document and provides feedback.

and improve group dynamics and interaction among all students and between the instructor and the students:

- Make sure you (the instructor) and students are familiar with the technological environment (hardware and software) before starting the course. Organize a workshop in advance and provide students with tutorial documents or videos.
- Provide students with protocols on *"What to do if . . ."* for common issues that may arise (video conference software not working; audio not working in a listening exercise; lack of some materials).
- Backup technology. Have backup software/hardware in case something goes wrong (e.g., video conference software and hardware on another device; collaborative tools).
- Backup communication tools. If the audio/video is not working, make sure there is a backup channel (email, chat) so the communication between the instructor and remote students is not broken and students know what protocol to follow.
- Making audio and video files available. When planning on showing a video or listening to an audio file, make sure students can access it on their own if possible. In that way, if there is a technical issue remote students can listen to it on their own and then resume the connection after everyone has listened to it.

- Provide students with a class plan or a list of activities in advance. In case there is a technological problem, remote students can continue working on their own while the instructor solves the problem.
- When addressing students in class, alternate between face-to-face and remote students, trying to balance the interaction among the two groups.
- The blackboard, that old friend. Analog tools can be very useful when technology breaks down. If the audio of the video conference system is interrupted, the blackboard can be used to write messages to remote students.
- Make sure to provide students with one-on-one time and attention. This can be done synchronously or asynchronously.
- Email can be very useful in following-up with students after class and even in establishing bonds that can be more difficult to have with remote students in BSL environments. Communication between instructor and students outside of the classroom in BSL environments is more essential than in face-to-face courses.
- Online office hours are a great way of having one-on-one moments with students (especially with remote students). Instead of "online office hours," they can be renamed in a more inviting way, or they can be compulsory individual meetings held periodically for remote students (though they benefit face-to-face students as well).

Conclusion

Throughout this book, our goal has been to give language instructors, administrators, and support staff the information we wish we had before we started teaching languages in blended synchronous environments. We have given an overview of the concerns that need to be considered before beginning BSL courses and some pedagogical practices that can help optimize language teaching in this challenging setting. But this book is intended to be a starting point, not a definitive road map. Advancements in technology and subsequent effects on users' expectations mean that BSL environments will be constantly evolving. By combining the principles outlined in this book with passion and creativity, we hope language educators will continuously find new and engaging ways to bring students from remote locations into their classrooms.

References

Bell, John, William Cain, Amy Peterson, and Cui Cheng. 2016. "From 2D to Kubi to Doubles: Designs for Student Telepresence in Synchronous Hybrid Classrooms." *International Journal of Designs for Learning* 7 (3): 19–33.

Bell, John, William Cain, and Sandra Sawaya. "Introducing the Role of Technology Navigator in a Synchromodal Learning Environment." In *Proceedings of EdMedia 2013—World Conference on Educational Media and Technology*, edited by Jan Herrington, Alec Couros, and Valerie Irvine, 1629–34. Chesapeake, VA: Association for the Advancement of Computing in Education, 2013.

Bell, John, Sandra Sawaya, and William Cain. 2014. "Synchromodal Classes: Designing for Shared Learning Experiences between Face-to-Face and Online Students." *International Journal of Designs for Learning* 5 (1): 68–82.

Bower, Matt, Barney Dalgarno, Gregor E. Kennedy, Mark J. W. Lee, and Jacqueline Kenney. 2015. "Design and Implementation Factors in Blended Synchronous Learning Environments: Outcomes from a Cross-Case Analysis." *Computers & Education* 86 (August): 1–17.

Bower, Matt, Barney Dalgarno, Gregor Kennedy, Mark J. W. Lee, Jacqueline Kenney, and Blended Synchronous Learning Project. 2014. *Blended Synchronous Learning: A Handbook for Educators*. Sydney, Australia: Department of Education.

Butz, Nikolaus T., Robert H. Stupnisky, Erin S. Peterson, and Melissa M. Majerus. 2014. "Motivation in Synchronous Hybrid Graduate Business Programs: A Self-Determination Approach to Contrasting Online and On-Campus Students." *Journal of Online Learning and Teaching* 10 (2): 211–27.

Cain, William, Sandra Sawaya, and John Bell. "Innovating the Hybrid Small Group Model in a SynchroModal Learning Environment." In *Proceedings of*

EdMedia 2013—World Conference on Educational Media and Technology, edited by Jan Herrington, Alec Couros, and Valerie Irvine, 1333–39. Chesapeake, VA: Association for the Advancement of Computing in Education, 2013.

Chakraborty, Mou, and Shelley Victor. 2004. "Do's and Don'ts of Simultaneous Instruction to On-Campus and Distance Students via Videoconferencing." *Journal of Library Administration* 41 (1–2): 97–112.

Conklin, Sheri. "Students' Perceptions of Interactions in a Blended Synchronous Learning Environment: A Case Study." PhD diss., Boise State University, 2017. https://doi.org/10.18122/B23M3W.

Conklin, Sheri, Beth Oyarzun, and Daisyane Barreto. 2017. "Blended Synchronous Learning Environment: Student Perspectives." *Research on Education and Media* 9 (1): 17–23.

Cunningham, Una. 2014. "Teaching the Disembodied: Othering and Activity Systems in a Blended Synchronous Learning Situation." *The International Review of Research in Open and Distributed Learning* 15 (6): 33–51.

Dörnyei, Zoltán, and Angi Malderez. 1997. "Group Dynamics and Foreign Language Teaching." *System* 25 (1): 65–81.

Dörnyei, Zoltán, and Tim Murphey. 2003. *Group Dynamics in the Language Classroom.* Cambridge: Cambridge University Press.

Hastie, Megan, I-Chun Hung, Nian-Shing Chen, and Kinshuk. 2010. "A Blended Synchronous Learning Model for Educational International Collaboration." *Innovations in Education and Teaching International* 47 (1): 9–24.

Popov, Oleg. 2009. "Teachers' and Students' Experiences of Simultaneous Teaching in an International Distance and On-Campus Master's Programme in Engineering." *The International Review of Research in Open and Distributed Learning* 10 (3): 1–17.

Rogers, P. Clint, Charles R. Graham, Rus Rasmussen, J. Olin Campbell, and Donna M. Ure. 2003. "Blending Face-to-Face and Distance Learners in a Synchronous Class: Instructor and Learner Experiences." *Quarterly Review of Distance Education* 4 (3): 245–51.

Roseth, Cary, Mete Akcaoglu, and Andrea Zellner. 2013. "Blending Synchronous Face-to-Face and Computer-Supported Cooperative Learning in a Hybrid Doctoral Seminar." *TechTrends* 57 (3): 54–59.

Stewart, Anissa R., Danielle B. Harlow, and Kim DeBacco. 2011. "Students' Experience of Synchronous Learning in Distributed Environments." *Distance Education* 32 (3): 357–81.

Szeto, Elson. 2014. "A Comparison of Online/Face-to-Face Students' and Instructor's Experiences: Examining Blended Synchronous Learning Effects." *Procedia - Social and Behavioral Sciences* 116 (February): 4250–54.

———. 2015. "Community of Inquiry as an Instructional Approach: What Effects of Teaching, Social and Cognitive Presences Are There in Blended Synchronous Learning and Teaching?" *Computers & Education* 81 (February): 191–201.

Szeto, Elson, and Annie Y. N. Cheng. 2016. "Towards a Framework of Interactions in a Blended Synchronous Learning Environment: What Effects are There on Students' Social Presence Experience?" *Interactive Learning Environments* 24 (3): 487–503.

University of Wisconsin. n.d. "Collaborative Language Program." https://www.wisconsin.edu/collaborative-language-program/.

Wang, Qiyun, and Changqin Huang. 2018. "Pedagogical, Social and Technical Designs of a Blended Synchronous Learning Environment: Designs of a Blended Synchronous Learning Environment." *British Journal of Educational Technology* 49 (3): 451–62.

About the Authors

Alba Girons has a PhD in translation and intercultural studies from the Autonomous University of Barcelona. She has lived and taught in Spain, France, and the United States (Georgetown University and the University of Chicago), both in secondary and higher education. Passionate about the impact of technology in the learning process, she has been offering her Catalan courses in blended synchronous environments since 2015.

Nicholas Swinehart is an instructional technologist and researcher at the University of Chicago, specializing in language pedagogy, assessment, and coordinating technological and administrative aspects of blended synchronous language courses. His previous publications include chapters in the *Handbook of Research on Mobile Technology, Constructivism, and Meaningful Learning* and the *Handbook of Research on Learner-Centered Pedagogy in Teacher Education and Professional Development*.

CPSIA information can be obtained
at www.ICGtesting.com
Printed in the USA
BVHW030031130120
569153BV00001B/6/P

9 781626 168060